WHOLE WIDE WORLD

PARTHENON

by Kristine Spanier, MLIS

pogo

Ideas for Parents and Teachers

Pogo Books let children practice reading informational text while introducing them to nonfiction features such as headings, labels, sidebars, maps, and diagrams, as well as a table of contents, glossary, and index.

Carefully leveled text with a strong photo match offers early fluent readers the support they need to succeed.

Before Reading

- "Walk" through the book and point out the various nonfiction features. Ask the student what purpose each feature serves.
- Look at the glossary together. Read and discuss the words.

Read the Book

- Have the child read the book independently.
- Invite him or her to list questions that arise from reading.

After Reading

- Discuss the child's questions. Talk about how he or she might find answers to those questions.
- Prompt the child to think more. Ask: The Parthenon was built for Athena. She was in Greek myths. Do you know any myths?

Pogo Books are published by Jump!
5357 Penn Avenue South
Minneapolis, MN 55419
www.jumplibrary.com

Library of Congress Cataloging-in-Publication Data

Names: Spanier, Kristine, author.
Title: Parthenon / by Kristine Spanier.
Description: Minneapolis, MN: Jump!, Inc., [2021]
Series: Whole wide world | Includes index.
Audience: Ages 7-10 | Audience: Grades 2-3
Identifiers: LCCN 2020028526 (print)
LCCN 2020028527 (ebook)
ISBN 9781645277446 (hardcover)
ISBN 9781645277453 (paperback)
ISBN 9781645277460 (ebook)
Subjects: LCSH: Parthenon (Athens, Greece)
Juvenile literature. | Athens (Greece)
Buildings, structures, etc.–Juvenile literature.
Classification: LCC NA281 .S63 2021 (print)
LCC NA281 (ebook) | DDC 726/.120809385–dc23
LC record available at https://lccn.loc.gov/2020028526
LC ebook record available at https://lccn.loc.gov/2020028527

Editor: Jenna Gleisner
Designer: Molly Ballanger

Photo Credits: Martina Badini/Shutterstock, cover; Dpikros/Dreamstime, 1; risteski goce/Shutterstock, 3; Rawf88/Dreamstime, 4; North Wind Picture Archives/Alamy, 5; DeAgostini/SuperStock, 6-7, 9; Yes058/Shutterstock, 8; Luckyphotographer/Dreamstime, 10-11; Viacheslav Lopatin/Shutterstock, 12-13 (top); Markara77/Dreamstime, 12-13 (bottom); Veja/Shutterstock, 14 (hands); INTERFOTO/Alamy, 14 (screen); Edwin Remsberg/age fotostock/SuperStock, 15; Juan Carlos Muñoz/age fotostock/SuperStock, 16-17; Gino Santa Maria/Shutterstock, 18-19tl; Joe Ravi/Shutterstock, 18-19tr; Coitelada/Shutterstock, 18-19bl; Resul Muslu/Shutterstock, 18-19br; Scaliger/Dreamstime, 20-21; Kollawat Somsri/Shutterstock, 23.

Printed in the United States of America, Fargo, ND.

TABLE OF CONTENTS

CHAPTER 1

A TEMPLE FOR ATHENA

A hill rises above Athens, Greece. It is more than 500 feet (152 meters) tall. At the top are **ruins**. This is called the Acropolis. The Parthenon is here.

Athens was named for Athena. She was a Greek goddess. Pericles was a leader of Athens. He wanted to **honor** Athena. How? He ordered a **temple** to be built.

Construction began in 447 BCE. It took nine years to complete. People call it the finest example of Greek **architecture**.

DID YOU KNOW?

A statue of Athena once stood inside. It was 30 feet (9 m) tall! It was made of ivory and gold. What happened to it? Nobody knows!

Parthenon

CHAPTER 2

GREEK ARCHITECTURE

The Parthenon is made of marble. More than 100,000 tons (90,718 metric tons) were used. The Greeks brought it from a **quarry**. Oxen pulled it in carts.

It was painted. Parts were red, blue, and green. Over time, it faded. Now it is white.

There are 46 columns on the outside. Each is 34 feet (10 m) tall. Each one had 20 grooves carved in. These are called flutes. The columns are more than six feet (1.8 m) around.

TAKE A LOOK!

The column style is called Doric. Greeks used two other kinds. One was Ionic. The other was Corinthian. Compare each style. What do you notice?

A triangular space is under the roof. This is called a pediment. Carved figures showed Greek **myths**.

Inside the temple was a **frieze**. It ran along the top. It showed Greek people and gods.

DID YOU KNOW?

Phidias was a famous **sculptor** at the time. He designed how the sculptures should look.

pediment

frieze

CHAPTER 3

LASTING INFLUENCE

The building was a temple for Athena until the 400s. It then became a meeting place for other religions. In the 1600s, **ammunition** was stored inside. It exploded during a battle. Parts were destroyed.

The Ottoman **Empire** ruled Athens starting in the mid-1400s. Its rule lasted until 1821. The building was not protected. People took marble to build homes. Visitors also took pieces.

From 1802 to 1812, Lord Elgin took many of the sculptures. He was a British **ambassador**. He sold them to the British Museum. They are called the Elgin Marbles.

A museum is nearby in Athens. Visitors can see copies of what was once here.

WHAT DO YOU THINK?

People of Greece want the **artifacts** back. Do you think they should be returned? Why or why not?

Parthenon,
Nashville, TN, USA

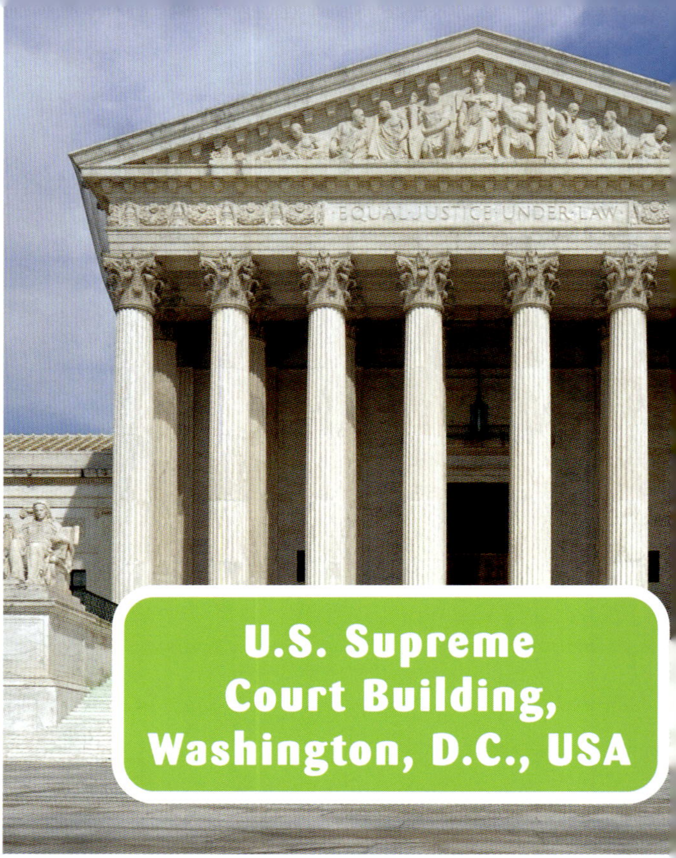

U.S. Supreme
Court Building,
Washington, D.C., USA

Maison Carrée,
Nîmes, France

Pantheon,
Rome, Italy

The Parthenon has **influenced** other buildings around the world. Some are in Europe. Others are in the United States. An exact copy is in Tennessee!

WHAT DO YOU THINK?

Have you seen a building that looks like this? Where was it? What was the same? What was different?

People now work to save the building. Why? It is important to remember its history. People from around the world visit. Would you like to see it?

QUICK FACTS & TOOLS

AT A GLANCE

PARTHENON

Location: Athens, Greece

Size: 23,028 square feet (2,139 square meters)

Years Built: 447 to 438 BCE

Primary Architects: Ictinus and Callicrates

Sculptor: Phidias

Past Use: temple

Current Use: cultural site and visitor attraction

Number of Visitors Each Year: around 2 million

GLOSSARY

ambassador: Someone sent by a government to represent it in another country.

ammunition: Objects such as bullets or shells that can be fired from weapons.

architecture: A style of building.

artifacts: Objects made or changed by humans, especially those from the past.

empire: A group of countries or states that have the same ruler.

frieze: A band or area around a building that is used for decoration.

honor: To show respect.

influenced: Had an effect on someone or something.

myths: Old stories that express the beliefs or history of a group of people or explain natural events.

quarry: A place where stone, slate, or sand is taken.

ruins: The remains of something that has collapsed or been destroyed.

sculptor: A person who carves or shapes something out of stone, wood, marble, or clay.

temple: A building used for worship.

INDEX

TO LEARN MORE

Finding more information is as easy as 1, 2, 3.

1. Go to www.factsurfer.com
2. Enter "Parthenon" into the search box.
3. Choose your book to see a list of websites.

FACT SURFER